Streets of London

Kevin McCormack

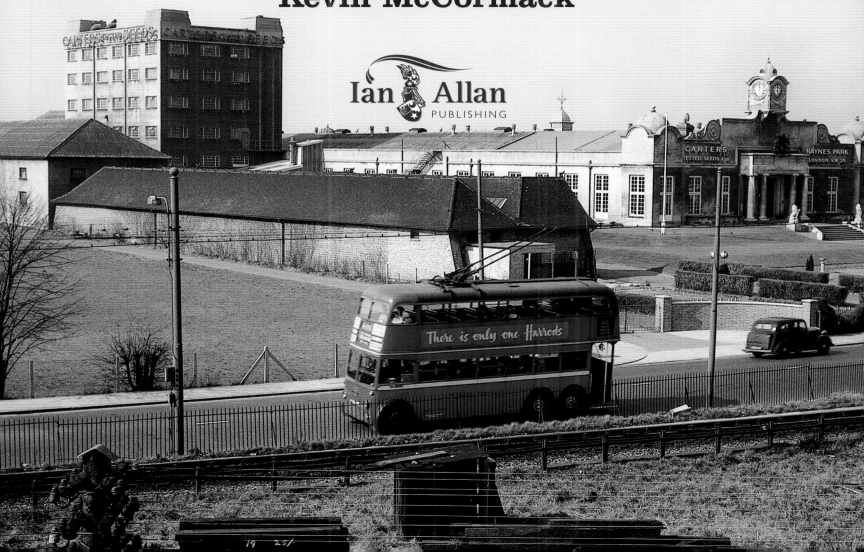

Ian Allan PUBLISHING

Introduction

The focus of this title, *Streets of London*, is the portrayal, in colour, of the capital's trams, trolleybuses and motor buses in postwar scenes which convey the atmosphere of the era.

All but two of the photographs were taken between 1945 and 1962, the latter date marking the cessation of 31 years of trolleybus operation in London.

Trolleybuses were introduced primarily to replace trams because, having electric traction, they were able to use much of the tram infrastructure. The electric tram, successor of the horse tram, had entered London service in 1901, but, despite upgrading and the introduction of some new vehicles, the system was, by the mid-1930s, becoming time-expired and inconvenient. Trams normally travelled down the centre of the road, causing traffic congestion and risking passenger safety. Trolleybuses, not being confined to rails, offered increased speed and comfort, as well as being able to pull up, like buses, at the kerb. But alas, like trams, they could not overtake one another.

The tram-to-trolleybus conversion programme would have been completed by the early 1940s but for the outbreak of World War 2 in 1939. By the time the war ended in 1945, the greater flexibility of bus operation, independent of fixed poles and wires, had been clearly demonstrated. London Transport ('LT') therefore decided that the remaining trams should be replaced by diesel buses. But first, a start had to be made on refurbishing and renewing the largely obsolete and non-standard bus fleet. Meanwhile, the trams, some of which were by now over 40 years old, soldiered on, mainly in areas south of the Thames, their final glory being to assist in taking visitors to the Festival of Britain on the South Bank in 1951. Final withdrawal came in July 1952 — or perhaps we should say temporary withdrawal, for London now has a tram system once more. On 10 May 2000, Fred Roberts, who drove Croydon's last tram on the night of 6/7 April 1951, helped to inaugurate the new Croydon Tramlink service, which extends to Wimbledon, Elmers End, Beckenham and New Addington. However, the new continental-style trams are a far cry from yesteryear's rattlers, which had to be driven standing up and, until 1930, without even the luxury of windscreens.

Soon after the demise of the trams, attention turned to the future of the trolleybus system, the largest in Britain, but now also showing its age. The first task of the legendary Routemaster bus, which was in production from 1958 to 1968, was to replace the trolleybus; it would then start replacing its immediate predecessors, buses of the RT family. No one, of course, could have foreseen that some of those trolleybus-replacement Routemasters would still be in regular service in London over 40 years later.

It is not easy to capture the early postwar period in colour, because colour film was still largely in its infancy at that time and was both expensive and often inflexible to use. Nevertheless,

Title page:
The long demolished Carters Seeds headquarters in West Barnes Lane, Raynes Park, seen in all its glory from Bushey Road bridge in early 1962. The 605 trolleybus is on its way from nearby Wimbledon to Teddington. *Marcus Eavis*

Right:
This autumnal view *c*1961 depicts RT1318 in Eaton Rise, Ealing, at the junction of Montpelier Avenue and Montpelier Road. Childhood memories are evoked, for the bus is approaching the author's old school. *Author*

First published 2001
Reprinted 2002, 2003 and 2005
This impression 2006

ISBN 0 7110 2774 9

Published by Ian Allan Publishing

an imprint of Ian Allan Publishing Ltd, Hersham, Surrey KT12 4RG.
Printed by Ian Allan Printing Ltd, Hersham, Surrey KT12 4RG.

Code: 0609/A

through various helpful contacts, I have managed to find material of suitable quality which is either previously unpublished or at least has not been seen before in large, uncropped format.

The book has roughly been divided equally between the three types of road transport covered, and I have C. Carter to thank for providing all the individual tram photographs. It has been a privilege to be able to use so many of his remarkable pre-1953 Dufays, which complement his unique provincial bus material published in *Heyday of the Bus: the Postwar Years*.

Thanks to an introduction by John Gent of the Croydon Natural History & Scientific Society, I have been fortunate to meet Harold Bennett, former World War 2 pilot and retired professional photographer. It has proved impossible to resist using his well-known 1945 image of a bus squeezing alongside a tram near Allders department store in Croydon, yet the accompanying view taken from a first floor window has not, to my knowledge, been seen before. Over 55 years later, Harold Bennett enjoys experimenting with the latest computer technology and generously agreed to colour three black and white photographs which are included in this book. It was a burdensome task but the technique offers exciting prospects for the future.

Other photographers I must thank for their valuable contributions are Geoff Rixon, Bruce Jenkins, Marcus Eavis, Trevor Saunders, Roy Hobbs, Bill Godwin and John Aldridge. Photographs from the Frank Hunt collection are held by the Light Rail Transit Association, London Area. Thanks also to Mike Burgess, Tony Beard, Jef Johnson, Jim Joyce and Geoff Morant.

One of the delights of compiling this book was making visits to many of the locations to witness the changes which have taken place over the years (half a century in many cases). This job was made much easier thanks to Ulrike Schrenk and Judith Barnes tramping the streets with me and accepting the discomforts of travelling in my 1932 and 1957 Austins.

As usual, I have relied on various publications for information on vehicles, routes, etc, in particular: *London's Trams Then and Now* by Julian Thompson (Ian Allan, 1992), *London Tramways* by John Reed (Capital Transport, 1997), *London Trolleybus Routes* by Hugh Taylor (Capital Transport, 1994) and *London Trams in Camera* by Julian Thompson (Ian Allan, 1971).

I now invite readers to take an historical journey through London's central (red bus) area. You will enter a more relaxed world

where there is little traffic, minimal road markings and definitely no graffiti, fast-food shops or baseball caps!

Kevin R. McCormack
Ashtead, Surrey
May 2001

Left:
This view outside the Odeon Cinema in Hill Street, Richmond was probably taken in the early days of the war (September 1939). The bus — ST806 dating from 1931 — and the Humber car are fitted with headlight shields, and some of the people are carrying gas masks. While the Belisha beacon and bus stop have gone, the cinema survives (complete with canopy), as do the dome on the extreme left and clock (albeit slightly altered) and the building with the advertisements. *Mike Burgess collection*

Above:
'Prewar' RT47, on driver-training duties, and an FX3-type taxi have Piccadilly to themselves in this 1958 view taken at Green Park station. On the right, with its Parisienne-style pavement colonnade, stands the famous Ritz Hotel, completed in 1906. This scene has changed little today and the car showroom is still extant.
Marcus Eavis

Above:
Seven weeks of industrial action in 1958 brought about the permanent withdrawal of 19 Central Area bus routes, including lowbridge route 127. 'Regent Low Height' RLH67 is seen at the offending bridge at Worcester Park, on the Waterloo to Epsom railway line. The road was lowered in 1963 after a replacement bridge was installed, but otherwise the scene is much the same today. *Bruce Jenkins*

Right:
At North Finchley in June 1959, trolleybus 294 dating from 1936 displays the smart rear wheel spats which were fitted to one hundred of the 'C' class. Route 645 was withdrawn on 2 January 1962, which coincided with a rare bout of snowy weather. *Bruce Jenkins*

Elephant & Castle changed almost beyond recognition in the 1960s and is due for another makeover shortly. These views were taken outside the vanished pub of that name on 11 November 1950 and 2 July 1950 respectively. Tram No 1798 *(above)* is an elderly 'E1' type with lower-deck reinforcement struts, contrasting with the modern lines of ex-Metropolitan No 2119 *(right)*, a 'Feltham'-type tram dating from 1931: an STL bus approaches on route 133. *(both) C. Carter*

Left:
Built in 1909 and still carrying its pre-1914 route colour-code lights above the destination blind is 'E1' No 1316, seen with 'Feltham' tram No 2107 on 22 August 1950. South London House (70/72 London Road) is the sole survivor of the buildings at the Elephant & Castle portrayed in this book, and now occupies a corner site. The building which incorporates the Bakerloo Line station, was designed by Leslie Green for the Underground and built in 1914. *C. Carter*

Above:
Tram No 117 belonged to the 'HR2' ('Hilly Route') class and operated exclusively on the sub-ground conduit system, being one of a batch with no overhead equipment. It is seen on 14 May 1950 in Short Street (between Walworth Road and Newington Butts) — a site since obliterated by a shopping precinct — and is heading for the more prestigious area around the Savoy Hotel in the Strand. *C. Carter*

Left:
This is Elephant & Castle on 24 July 1949, showing former East Ham No 69 (LT No 99) dating from 1928, and still carrying an enamel side advertisement. Beyond is former Leyton Council No 162, built in 1930. A STL bus stands on the extreme left.
C. Carter (coloured by Harold Bennett)

Above:
Vehicle shortages arising from the war caused LT to break with tradition and purchase two batches of Bristol buses. Now rapidly approaching the end of its career in London is B16, built in 1946 and photographed in March 1953 pulling away from Ealing Broadway District Line station (rebuilt in 1910 and still extant today). *Geoff Rixon*

Showing what a difference a few weeks can make, 'L3' class trolleybus No 1433 waits at Hampton Court on 20 April 1962 *(left),* just 2½ weeks before new buses such as RM1210, standing at the same stop, took over *(right)*. *Geoff Rixon*

Dating from 5 November 1961, two days before the end of trolleybus operation in Central London, these photographs were taken at Chancery Lane Underground station and depict trolleybuses 1512 *(left)* and 1467 *(above)* entering/exiting Gray's Inn Road at its junction with High Holborn. In the background stands Staple Inn, an Elizabethan structure which survived the Great Fire of London in 1666 through being just outside its range. The obelisk (now altered) marks the City of London boundary; the War Memorial commemorates the fallen of the Royal Fusiliers (City of London Regiment). *Trevor Saunders*

Left:
Some Central Area (red) bus routes ran well into the countryside, in this case 15½ miles from London, according to the signpost. TD87 comes to the end of Ongar Road at Passingford Bridge, Essex, while working route 250 in 1958. *Marcus Eavis*

Above:
Surplus to requirements when built in 1954 and subsequently stored, RTL1585 had just entered service when seen here in April 1958 at the eastern end of the Strand. Behind the bus stop stands the Church of St Clement Danes, and beyond that are the Law Courts. *Marcus Eavis*

A scene outside 255 McLeod Road (still extant) on 30 April 1950 as 'E1' No 1533 and ex-West Ham No 344 proceed towards Abbey Wood's Knee Hill terminus around the corner.

The background is now occupied by a roundabout leading to a flyover, which enabled the level crossing beside the railway station to be abandoned. *C. Carter*

At the terminus on 29 June 1952, ex-East Ham No 84 proclaims Last Tram Week. Curiously, while this vehicle is standing in London, the others are actually in Kent, the boundary running between the tram tracks! The building on the right is the hall, now condemned, belonging to The Harrow pub on the corner of Abbey Road. The former tram shelter for passengers, located on the photographer's left, still survives. *C. Carter*

London's first 8ft-wide public service vehicles were 43 trolleybuses built between 1941 and 1943 which were destined for South Africa but not exported due to wartime risks to shipping. Because of their extra width (and weight) they needed special dispensation to operate and were all concentrated at Ilford depot. No 1747 heads a column of three at Barkingside in November 1958 *(above)*, and No 1750 passes No 1738 as it pulls out of Hainault Street into Ilford High Road *(right)*. The General Havelock public house remains relatively unchanged today. *Bruce Jenkins; Frank Hunt collection*

Dating from 1947, RT458 heads down Hainault Street into Ilford High Road pursued by a bright blue bubblecar. The date is 30 June 1962, nearly three years after the trolleybus wires were removed.

All the buildings visible are still standing today, but there is no evidence of John Collier or Pearl Assurance. *Trevor Saunders*

Back in the electric era, South African (Durban) trolleybus No 1723 stands at Chadwell Heath in 1955. The trolleybuses destined for Durban had darkened windows unlike those for Johannesburg, such as the vehicle behind. *Frank Hunt*

Above:
'L3' class trolleybus No 1427 and a Morris 8 car cross the River Crane on the approach to Twickenham station. The old-fashioned butcher's shop is now a unisex hair salon. The author can remember that in the 1960's the tram tracks were visible through the tarmac of the road just further along from here. *Geoff Rixon*

Right:
In this summer 1959 view, a traffic policeman surveys the River Thames from Tower Bridge, while RT721 passes by on its way from Shoreditch to Dulwich. Tower Bridge was built in 1894 in Gothic style and has a central section which lifts to allow the passage of tall vessels. On the left stands the Tower of London, a former Royal fortress, parts of which date back to the 11th century. *Marcus Eavis*

Left:
Recognisable by the lower-deck double-width central pillar is this 'E1' tram from the 50-strong batch reconstructed from single-deckers in 1930. This shot was taken on 10 June 1950 outside Waterloo station (behind the photographer). Only the building then occupied by Chamberlain Yacht Stores survives today. *C. Carter*

Above:
This tram belongs to the 'E3' class — flush-sided metal-bodied cars built in 1930 to operate through the rebuilt Kingsway Subway, which had been enlarged to accommodate double-decker trams. *C. Carter*

Above:

The last London bus to remain in service in the old red and cream livery was Brixton's RT2495. Its final public run before repaint into all-red livery was on 22 May 1955, and this view on the south side of Southwark Bridge was taken a few days earlier. The ultra-modern *Financial Times* building now stands in place of the Grey & Marten premises. Even the red telephone box has been replaced by a modern version. *Bruce Jenkins*

Right:

All but two of the 127 postwar 'Q1' class trolleybuses were sold to Spain in 1961, thereby advancing the abandonment of the London trolleybus network by several years. The 'Q1s' had been due to remain in service until the late 1960s. This August 1957 view shows No 1788 pulling out of St Mark's Hill into Claremont Road by Surbiton station. Today, the parade of shops remains extant but the array of blinds has sadly disappeared; the chemist's is now an estate agent's. *Bruce Jenkins*

This is East India Dock Road, looking east from the corner of Annabel Close. Vehicles in this early postwar view include RTL502, trolleybus No 1483, a Dodge lorry and a Morris GPO telephone van. Nothing has changed here in 50 years, but Canary Wharf tower now rises up over the photographer's right shoulder. No 133 East India Dock Road and its stone 'cruets' (on the left of the picture) have recently been repainted white and look splendid; No 154 (opposite) is the former Missions to Seamen Institute. The hanging clock behind the trolleybus pole is still extant, along with the trees and 'back to front' houses on the right. *LT Museum*

In this early-1950s scene, a 1935 Morris 8 leads RT2375 out of Victoria Street into Broad Sanctuary and thence into Parliament Square. A new Austin FX3 taxi shares the road with two prewar models. The monument on the right of the picture was erected in 1861 and dedicated to former pupils of Westminster School who died in the Russian and Indian wars, 1854-9. To its right is the since-cleaned-up frontage of Westminster Abbey dating from 1738/9. On the extreme right, at the corner of Great Smith Street, is Westminster Chambers, built in 1854, with its unusual oriel window. Behind St Margaret's church stands the Clock Tower of the Gothic-style Houses of Parliament (built 1840-57). The tower houses Big Ben, the bell named after Sir Benjamin Hall, First Commissioner of Works at the time it was cast.

The view today is not greatly different, apart from the London Eye (Millennium Wheel) spanning the gap between the trees.
LT Museum

Left:
This busy scene in Brixton Hill on 7 April 1951 depicts 'Feltham' tram No 2129 working as an extra alongside an RT-type bus. Ninety of the 100 'Felthams' were sold to Leeds for further service. On the left is Brixton Town Hall, built in 1906; the domed building on the corner of Acre Lane is today the inevitable fast-food outlet. *C. Carter*

Above:
The last survivors of the 131-strong TD class operated from Edgware garage, and TD104 is seen passing under the low bridge at Mill Hill station on 7 October 1962 during its last few days in passenger service. *Bruce Jenkins*

Above:
The 'prewar' RTs were withdrawn from Central Area service on 31 May 1955. Six days earlier, three of the class (RT50 in front) plus a postwar model were photographed at Epsom Downs, having brought Derby Day punters from Morden Underground station.
Bruce Jenkins

Right:
Here we see passengers boarding a wartime Guy Austerity bus in Queen Victoria Street, near Puddle Dock, during the eight-year reign of this type on route 76, from 1942 to 1950. The Baynard

Castle pub still stands today, but has recently been renamed 'The Goose at the Castle'. The Church of St Andrew-by-the-Wardrobe was built by Sir Christopher Wren in 1685-95, the Great Fire of London having destroyed its predecessor. Gutted by enemy action in 1941, it was reconstructed in 1959-61, retaining the surviving tower and walls. 'Wardrobe' refers to the nearby former location of the warehouse containing the armour, robes etc of mediæval monarchs. An optical illusion is created by the headquarters of the British & Foreign Bible Society, dating from 1866 and now D'Arcy House (146 Queen Victoria Street): what appears to be the front of the building is in fact the side. *Bill Godwin*

Above:
This 1958 view of Anerley Road, with the Crystal Palace radio mast in the distance, features a 'B1'-type short trolleybus, No 66, built in 1935. This class was fitted with special braking apparatus for use on South London hilly route 654. *Marcus Eavis*

Above:
Tamworth Road, Croydon, now echoes once more to the sound of
trams. Until 1935, London's last open-top trams ran here. In this
view taken in March 1957, trolleybus No 457 is seen operating the
second-longest trolleybus route (at just over 14½ miles), from West
Croydon to Harlesden (College Park). *Bruce Jenkins*

Above:
Twilight descends on the tram terminus at Southwark Bridge on
5 November 1950, as 'E3' class No 164 takes a rest. The aftermath
of the war is still evidenced by the temporary ramps on the bridge
and the damaged roof of Cannon Street station. Following
rebuilding, Southwark bridge was opened for traffic by King
George V and Queen Mary on 6 June 1921. *C. Carter*

Right:
Five minutes after the cover picture was taken, the photographer
moved to the first floor of Wilson's Café, from where ex-Croydon
Corporation tram No 379 and a distant 'Feltham' can be seen.
   Despite an interval of some 55 years, half the retailers in Allders'
block still trade there: Allders, H. Samuel and Burton's (stone
frontage to left of Union flags — occupied since construction in
1926). The Scala Cinema, however, is no more, having reverted to
Allders store. Trees and benches now occupy this section of road,
following pedestrianisation. *Harold Bennett*

A long Country Area route which touched the London suburbs was the 470 from Dorking to Chelsham. This early postwar view shows The Rectory, 1 Addington Road, with an FJJ- registered STL pausing at the top of Sanderstead Hill. Of the 132 members of this batch of STLs, 125 were converted to take RT bodies, becoming SRTs, and the surplus bodies fitted to earlier vehicles.

Photographed and coloured by Harold Bennett

In the days when buses used to cross Bushy Park, wartime austerity Daimler D133 takes the short cut from Hampton Court to Teddington in May 1953. *Geoff Rixon (coloured by Harold Bennett)*

These views were taken on 14 May 1950 on the Victoria Embankment, in the shadow of Hungerford railway bridge.

Left:
Standing in front of Charing Cross Pier is ex-London United 'Feltham' tram No 2151, which entered service in 1930. Just visible in the background is Waterloo Bridge, built 1938-40. The pole supporting the traffic lights appears to survive today as a lamp-post. *C. Carter*

Above:
In comparison with the 'Feltham', the two 'E1' trams waiting on the other side of the bridge look positively antiquated, No 1806 of 1922 vintage requiring strengthening struts. Behind the trams stands Hungerford railway/footbridge, employing red brick sections from Brunel's Italianate-style pedestrian suspension bridge (demolished 1862, its chains being transferred to Clifton Suspension Bridge). Behind the bridge is the shot-tower (for making ammunition) which used to stand next to the Royal Festival Hall. *C. Carter*

Stamford Hill, near Totttenham, in North London is the location of this busy 1961 street scene. The new bus stop replacing the flag previously attached to the pole heralds the forthcoming withdrawal of the trolleybus routes. Nos 1105 and 1112 belonged to the 'K1' class, introduced in late 1938. *Marcus Eavis*

New concrete lamp-posts dominate this empty dual carriageway at Whipps Cross, near Walthamstow in North East London. 'K2' class trolleybus No 1311, dating from 1939, heads for Central London's fashionable parts, some 22 years later. *Marcus Eavis*

Left:
This is London Airport (now Heathrow) on a summer Sunday in
1958, when it was a magnet for sightseers. Visible in the
photograph, which was taken from the top of the Queen's Building,
are no fewer than 26 LT buses, all members of the RT family. Of
these, 21 (including the green RT in the foreground) have arrived
on excursion tours. Interestingly, the first three, from Kingston,
King's Cross and Hackney, represent the three different types of RT:
RT4608, RTL525 (Leyland) and RTW193 (wide Leyland). At the head
of the service buses stands RT2326 on route 140 to Mill Hill.
Marcus Eavis

Above:
This November 1961 view depicts RT1384 picking up passengers in
Parliament Street against the backdrop of Whitehall and its
government buildings. In this scene, virtually unchanged today, is
the Cenotaph, its base covered with Remembrance Day wreaths. The
Old War Office Building is behind, dating from 1906. On the far left
is the Treasury, while the RTW bus is about to pass the Foreign &
Commonwealth Office. *John Aldridge*

These two shots were taken on the last day of trolleybus operation, 8 May 1962, and show crowds waiting for the special commemorative run.

Above:
Less fortunate is Kingston garage and bus station which, despite being around 80 years old, was ignominiously demolished in August 2000. *Geoff Rixon*

Left:
Fulwell depot, once home to trams, was the birthplace of London's trolleybus system in 1931 and currently survives as a bus garage. Even the clock still works today. *Geoff Rixon*

Above and right:
The Commemorative run has now arrived at Kingston, led by trolleybus No 1 which was built in 1931 and withdrawn from public service in 1948 when the 'Q1s' arrived. It is first seen in Bridge Street, where John Lewis now stands (all buildings except Bentall's having been swept away), and then a little further on in Clarence Street (now pedestrianised, but with its buildings intact), at the junction with Fife Road. *Geoff Rixon*

Above:
Accompanying No 1 on the special run was Class L3 No 1521, dating from 1940. Complete with police motorcycle escort, the trolleybus has just left Kingston Bridge at a point which has become a road junction. *Geoff Rixon*

Right:
Heading in the opposite direction is No 1444, approaching Hampton Wick from Kingston Bridge. *Geoff Rixon*

Left:
In the days before compulsory motorcycle helmets, trolleybus No 1413 stands in Clarence Street Kingston outside the ubiquitous Co-op. At this point today, the vehicle would be leaving the pedestrianised section. Only the tall brick building on the left survives. *Frank Hunt collection*

Above:
A 1913-built Wolseley truck with solid tyres passes a 1931-built AEC Renown (LT165) while competing in the annual HCVC run to Brighton for historic commercial vehicles. This view of Clapham Common South in May 1964 scarcely looks any different today. *Author*

Above:

With the *Cutty Sark* tea clipper just around the corner and Greenwich's other famous attractions nearby, Church Street is crowded with tourists these days. The location has long since lost the dilapidated appearance evident here on 21 April 1951 when it was a tram terminus. Class E1 No 554 is another 1930 conversion from a single-decker. The scruffy buildings behind it have now been replaced, although that on the right is still a chemist's; the Harris building (on the far left) is currently undergoing major refurbishment. *C. Carter*

Right:

The prototype Green Line Routemaster coach, CRL4 (later RMC4) undergoes trials at Chiswick Works prior to its entry into service on 9 October 1957. A similar vehicle in this splendid, traditional livery can still be seen in Central London, working route 15. Of particular note in this photograph are the cream coloured trafficators and bullseye motif. *Bill Godwin*

Left:
No 1483 turns round at the former tram terminus (until 1938) at the Church of St John the Baptist, Barnet, on 5 November 1961, two days before withdrawal of the trolleybuses. A Wolseley 1500 and a Hillman Minx represent the motor car department. *Trevor Saunders*

Above:
Standing outside the stylish 1938-built Underground station at Uxbridge is AEC Regal T758 on its way to London Airport (renamed Heathrow Airport in 1966 when the British Airports Authority assumed responsibility from the Ministry of Aviation). Surplus RFs brought about the demise of this class in 1958 after only 12 years' service, and most were sold to Ceylon (now Sri Lanka). *LT Museum*

Above:
In the mid-1930s, a handful of trams were rebuilt with modern-looking domed roofs. One such vehicle was No 2, which consisted of a new body built on the chassis of No 1370, following an accident in June 1933. The South Circular Road at Eltham Common looks no different today, except that the 'prefabs' (temporary houses) have given way to common land. *C. Carter*

Right:
Taken on the same day, 21 April 1951, was this close-up of ex-East Ham No 54 (LT No 84) in Well Hall Road, Eltham, opposite the parish church of St John the Baptist. This vehicle also carries enamel advertisements. *C. Carter*

Left:
A web of wires fills the sky as a former Leyton Council 'E3' tram prepares to turn out of Well Hall Road. All the buildings survive including the discreet vintage toilets against the churchyard wall on the left. *C. Carter*

Above:
Around the corner from Burton's (now a fast-food outlet), another 'E3' tram, followed by a Co-op van, heads down Eltham High Street. This vista has also hardly changed, apart from the parish church regaining the top of its spire which had been damaged by a flying bomb on 29 August 1944. *C. Carter*

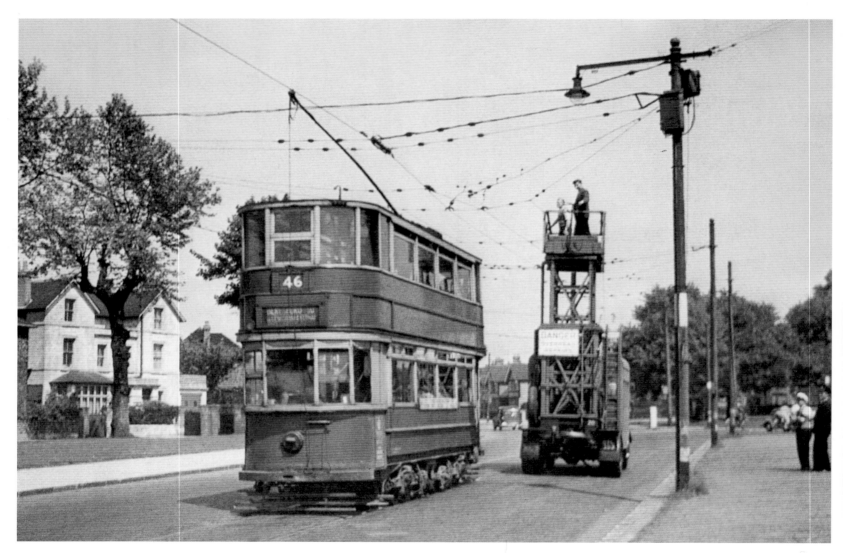

Mending the wires by the 'Yorkshire Grey' roundabout where the South Circular Road crosses the A210. Apart from the public house becoming a 'drive-through' burger establishment, the location looks the same today, with the houses at 1-2 Eltham Green being instantly recognisable. *C. Carter*

Further down Eltham Road, an 'E3' tram drops off some sportsmen.
The gap in the houses has now been filled by a modern
semi -detached house (6/7 Eltham Green). *C. Carter*

With work continuing on the overhead in the distance, former East Ham Corporation No 54 (LT No 100) waits in Eltham Road.

The large advertisement on the side of 13 Eltham Green is long gone. *C. Carter*

In the last days of London trolleybus operation, No 1474 travels along the fastest section on the system, where there were few stops and no trade: the eastern end of Hampton Court Road. *Bruce Jenkins*

Above:
Over half of the 76 members of the lowbridge RLH class were used in the Country (green bus) Area, and it was not uncommon for some to be drafted in as temporary cover on the three Central Area (red) routes which required low-height double-deckers. One such example was RLH22, photographed at Romford in May 1955. *Bruce Jenkins*

Right:
A 19th-century horsebus once used by the London General Omnibus Co gets an outing in Hyde Park for the 1959 Easter Parade. Behind it is the Spyker car which co-starred in the famous film, *Genevieve*. *Bruce Jenkins*

The furthest that trolleybuses ventured into Central London was Bloomsbury. Just short of this terminus, Class K1 No 1302 is seen in Theobald's Road in early April 1959, within days of withdrawal of route 555. The location is entirely recognisable today, even down to

the blue road sign and overhanging lamp, although the right turn to Holborn and Ludgate Circus has now been blanked out.
Roy Hobbs

In 1958, when this photograph was taken, Hounslow West was the terminus of the Piccadilly Line and the gateway to London (Heathrow) Airport, the 81B bus service (operated here by RT2284) providing the missing link to the Central Terminal Area. The station was originally called Hounslow Barracks, and the structure shown here was built in 1926. The provincial-looking AEC Regal I in the foreground is T749, dating from 1946. *Marcus Eavis*

Trams, trolleybuses and motorbuses all shared this section of Woolwich High Street near Ferry Approach. These two shots taken on 20 August 1950 show *(above)* unmodernised 'E1' tram No 1083, a veteran dating from 1908 and *(right)* former East Ham No 53 (LT No 83) waiting at the change pit where the underground conduit system (see the slot between the rails) gave way to overhead power. Today the scene is unrecognisable, due to the demolition of all the buildings, including the power station, and the re-alignment of the road. *C. Carter*

Left:
On 7 November 1950, rebuilt 'E1' No 1401 stands at the northern end of Southwark Bridge, the only tram terminus within the 'Square Mile' of the City of London. Today, only the top of the spire of Wren's St Michael Paternoster Royal (built 1690) remains visible from the bridge. The previous church on the site was destroyed in the Great Fire of London (1666) and allegedly contained the tomb of Dick Whittington, four times Lord Mayor of London between 1396 and 1419. *C. Carter*

Above:
The Aldgate terminus for buses, trolleybuses and Green Line coaches at the Minories was also in the City (just). In this view, Class L2 No 1374 joins other trolleybuses while a Green Line 10T10 stands in the shadows. Aldgate is the site of the erstwhile entrance to the City of London ('All-gate', ie open to all). *C. Carter*

Enfield was one of the few places where trolleybuses mingled with Country Area (green) buses. In this 1958 shot, No 841, dating from 1938, passes RT 4792, a mere four-year-old, but only recently placed in traffic. The line of cars consists of a Hillman Minx, an Austin A35 van, a Morris Minor and two Standards. *Marcus Eavis*

RF37, on a Green Line coach service to Guildford, displays its experimental livery of darker green relief around the windows and on the bullseye motif, in this unchanged scene at Esher on 26 August 1962. *Trevor Saunders*

Index of Locations

Front cover:

This remarkable photograph was taken on 1 September 1945 at North End, Croydon. STL255, of 1933 vintage, just manages to squeeze past 'E3' class tram No 1910, while another STL follows in the distance. On the right the former Hospital of the Holy Trinity, founded by Archbishop Whitgift in 1596 and unchanged today. *Harold Bennett*

Rear cover:

On 31 August 1961 the unique unpainted Routemaster, RM664, prepares to overtake RT2045 where Whitehall surreptitiously becomes Parliament Street. This creates the anomaly of two adjoining buildings on the east side being numbered 54 and 85! *Bruce Jenkins*

Full details of Ian Allan Publishing titles can be found on www.ianallanpublishing.com or by writing for a free copy of our latest catalogue to: Marketing Dept., Ian Allan Publishing, Riverdene Business Park, Molesey Road, Hersham KT12 4RG.

For an unrivalled range of aviation, military, transport and maritime publications, visit our secure on-line bookshop at www.ianallansuperstore.com

or visit the Ian Allan Bookshops in

Birmingham
47 Stephenson Street, B2 4DH;
Tel: 0121 643 2496; e-mail: bcc@ianallanpublishing.co.uk

Cardiff
31 Royal Arcade, CF10 1AE;
Tel: 02920 390615; e-mail: cardiff@ianallanpublishing.co.uk

London
45/46 Lower Marsh, Waterloo, SE1 7RG;
Tel: 020 7401 2100; e-mail: waterloo@ianallanpublishing.co.uk

Manchester
5 Piccadilly Station Approach, M1 2GH; Tel: 0161 237 9840;
e-mail: manchester@ianallanpublishing.co.uk

or through mail order by writing to:
Ian Allan Mail Order Dept.,
4 Watling Drive, Hinckley LE10 3EY.
Tel: 01455 254450.
Fax: 01455 233737.
e-mail: midlandbooks@compuserve.com

You are only a visit away from over 1,000 publishers worldwide.